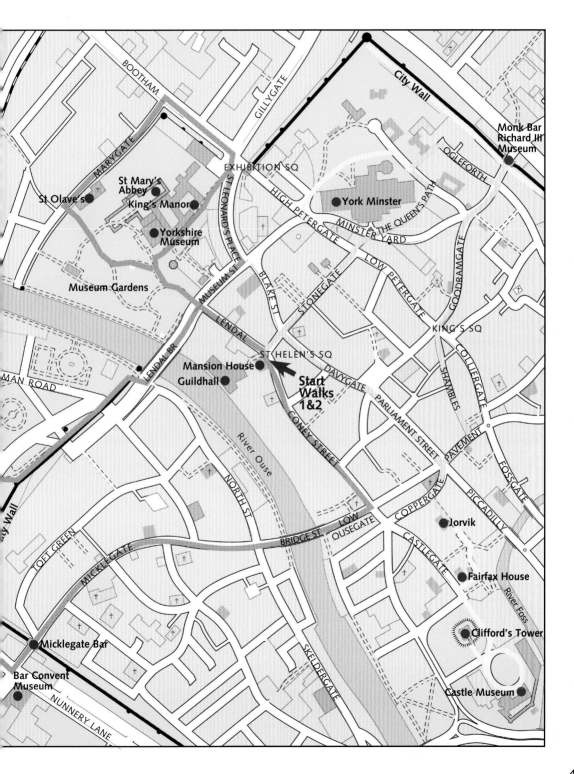

Welcome to York

York, encircled by ancient walls, its heart the historic stone Minster, is loved by visitors from around the world. This small city, built up layer by layer since Roman times by successive communities, has a rich history. As you walk the narrow streets with their evocative names, you'll discover little alleyways and connecting passages, known as snickelways, enticing you to explore further. For a wider view you can walk the city walls. The historic beauty is matched by 21st-century comforts – shops, theatres, cinemas, galleries, bookshops, pubs, restaurants and cafés. York is not a large city and visitors soon find their way around, enjoying both the ancient and the modern side-by-side.

A short history

The Romans, the Vikings and the Normans all made York their northern headquarters. For hundreds of years it was England's second city, a rich and prosperous port, superior in wealth and status to all except London.

The Romans called it 'Eboracum' and built defensive walls and a fortress where York Minster now stands. Constantine the Great, the first Christian emperor of Rome, was in York when he succeeded to his title. The next great invasion, that of the Vikings, happened about 450 years after the Romans withdrew. They called their new headquarters Jorvik, from which the name York derives. York's street names almost all originated with the Vikings.

Then came William the Conqueror in 1068. He quashed a rebellion, built himself a grand castle and flattened the city. The first Norman Minster, on the foundations of earlier stone churches, was begun in 1070. By the Middle Ages York, with its great River Ouse bringing trade and prosperity, was the most thriving town in the north of England. Many of the medieval and Tudor buildings survived the Reformation and the English Civil War. By the 18th century, York, no longer an international port, had become a large and busy market town and the focal point for northern society.

After the arrival of the railway and two chocolate companies, Terry's and Rowntree's, in the 19th century, the city prospered once more. The history not only of York, but also of England, is evident in the ancient buildings and the streets, walked by the millions of visitors who arrive each year to marvel at what the city has to offer.

St Helen's Square

All streets seem to lead to pedestrianized St Helen's Square, a natural meeting place with easy access to the River Ouse, York Minster, the Museum Gardens and the main shopping areas. St Helen was the mother of Constantine (see page 7) and there is a church named for her in the square. Imposing Georgian buildings, including the former showrooms and manufacturing base of chocolate-maker Terry's of York, line the square.

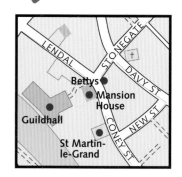

Bettys Café Tea Rooms

Bettys Café Tea Rooms

You'll see queues of people at the world-famous Bettys Tea Rooms – here and on Stonegate – the art deco stained glass, inspired by Cunard's Queen Mary, brightening one corner of the square. You are ushered to your table by traditionally dressed waitresses and faced with a bewildering choice of tea, coffee, patisserie and Yorkshire delicacies, such as Fat Rascals.

Viking names

Viking influence gave many York streets their names: the suffix 'gate', as in Stonegate, Petergate or Gillygate, comes from the Old Norse 'gata', meaning 'road' or 'path'.

Mansion House

York was able to boast that, even before London did, it provided a suitably grand residence for its Lord Mayor. The Mansion House, built between 1725 and 1730 at the end of Coney Street, where the chapel of the guild of St Christopher once stood, still houses the Lord Mayor and you'll see the city's coat of arms at the top of the building. The house, with its fine collection of silver, clocks and furniture, is open for public inspection on two days each week.

Mansion House

Guildhall

Turn down the narrow Mansion House arch and you'll find the ancient Guildhall, now home to much of York's city council. You are welcome to visit the hall, unless it's being used on council business. Most of the original 15th-century building, which once housed 50 merchant and craft guilds, including Cordwainers, Butchers and Scriveners, was destroyed by a wartime bomb in 1942. But the restoration is splendid, with its copies of the ancient roof bosses, wrought iron and painstakingly reconstructed stained glass. The Guildhall was once used as a law court and it was here, at the City Assizes of 1586, that York's now canonized Margaret Clitherow was condemned to a horrible death (see page 14).

Guildhall from the river

St Martin-le-Grand

St Martin-le-Grand

You can't fail to see the splendid clock, topped by a naval figure taking a reading from the sun, decorating this ancient church. St Martin-le-Grand, recorded in the Domesday Book, was badly damaged in the same bombing raid that hit the Guildhall. It's been partly restored and contains a magnificent 9.4-metre (31-foot) high stained-glass window that shows scenes from the life of St Martin of Tours.

Stonegate

York Minster lies ahead as you walk up Stonegate, one of York's prettiest roads. Here is medieval Mulberry Hall, decorated with woodcarving, and the Old Starre Inne (once Boddy's Star Inn), claiming to be the oldest alehouse in York. Originally the Via Praetoria of Roman York, Stonegate was the road up which the great stones to build York Minster were carted. Now it is paved with York stone and crammed with gift shops.

Printer's devil

Barley Hall

Printer's devil

Stonegate was renowned for its printing presses and book-shops. Under the eaves of No. 33 squats a little red devil, a reminder of the days when hot type was carried by lads known as 'devils'. A Bible above No. 35 denotes a one-time bookshop. Coffee Yard is the narrow 'snicket' (passageway) to Grape Lane. It was home to the coffee house where the printers and publishers would meet to discuss business.

Barley Hall

In 1984 the medieval town-house of Alderman William Snawsell, goldsmith and Mayor of York, was discov-ered. Barley Hall has been expertly rebuilt and you can wander through the rooms as they were in 1485, try on the kind of clothes they once wore and sit at the same kind of table. The Snawsell fam-ily lived here for 20 years. In 1540 the hall was confiscated by the Crown and divided into smaller properties.

Painted lady

This 17th-century ship's figurehead is a reminder of York's days as a flourishing riverside port.

Minster Yard

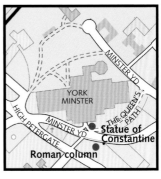

Cross High Petergate towards Minster Yard and look up to see Minerva, the goddess of wisdom, with her owl and books – an apt sign for the bookshop that was once here. Ahead is the south front and the entrance to the Minster, northern Europe's largest Gothic church and the fifth cathedral to be built here since the simple wooden structure erected to celebrate the baptism of Edwin, King of Northumbria in 627. It is dedicated to St Peter.

Statue of Emperor Constantine

Roman column

Ancient title

The official title of York Minster is 'the Cathedral and Metropolitical Church of St Peter in York'. 'Minster' reflects its role as a centre of Christian teaching or 'ministering'.

Statue of Emperor Constantine

The year was AD 306 and the Roman Emperor Constantius Chlorus lay dying in the Principia, his headquarters in the northern British garrison of Eboracum. He had subdued the barbarians, the Brigantes, helped by his son, Constantine. As his father died, Constantine seized power, donning the purple robes of office. Eboracum was the Roman name for York and it was here, on the site of the Minster, that Constantine became emperor. As the first Christian emperor of Rome, Constantine made Christianity the religion of Western Europe.

Roman column

The Romans had their garrison where the Minster now stands. Their great hall was supported by 36 stone columns, one of which was found during excavations in 1969 and can be seen across the way from the statue of Emperor Constantine.

York Minster

The Minster, built of pale limestone, with its three great towers, dominates the city of York. From vantage points on the city walls to glimpses all around the narrow streets, the great Gothic cathedral, built to rival that of Canterbury, is with you wherever you walk. Several churches have stood here since AD 627, but the foundations of what we see today were laid by Archbishop Walter de Grey in 1220. He died in 1255 and you can see his tomb in St Michael's Chapel in the graceful south transept, the first section of the cathedral to be completed. The work continued for almost 250 years.

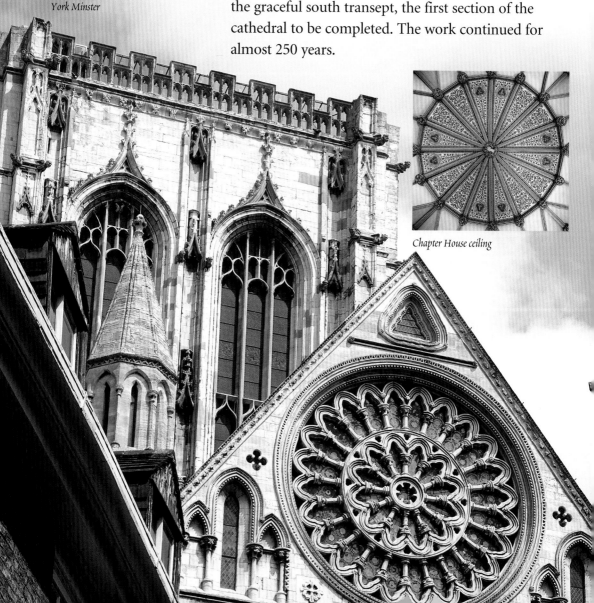

York Minster

Chapter House ceiling

The choir

All the major services are sung in the choir, which is enclosed by screens. The brass eagle lectern has been used for Bible readings since 1686. Don't miss the 36 panels in the north choir aisle stitched by members of the York Broderer's Guild, showing all the birds and animals depicted in the Minster.

Central tower

You may climb the 275 steps to the top of the 15th-century tower for a view over the city, or you can stand in the nave below and admire the central boss, depicting saints Peter and Paul.

North transept

There is much of interest in the north transept, just outside the Chapter House. Look for the striking clock with its two 400-year-old wooden figures, Gog and Magog, marking the hours and quarters by hitting each other. The modern astronomical clock is in memory of fallen airmen. Here, too, is the 'Five Sisters' window (see page 10).

Undercroft, treasury and crypt

Below ground are traces of the ancient Roman fortress. You'll also see Viking and Norman carvings, and church treasures and jewels. The crypt is still used for some special services and it is where St William of York lies buried.

The nave

The nave

The soaring height of the great Gothic arches, creating the widest nave in England, brings space, light and a feeling of intense spirituality. A spectacular 15th-century choir screen, dividing the nave from the choir, presents life-size figures of each of the 15 kings of England from William I to Henry VI. They bear an uncanny resemblance to each other.

Chapter House

Built primarily for business and not then a public space, the Chapter House is quite different in style from the rest of York Minster. Constructed in the Decorated style, you'll find elaborate carvings of heads, animals and leaves on the intricate stone canopies above the stalls. Green men, those symbols of life and rebirth, abound. The star-ribbed wooden roof, again richly decorated, soars above.

Gog and Magog, north transept

Dragon's head

Walk down the nave and peer upwards to see a dragon's head projecting from a gallery high above. This is actually a carved pivoted crane, which was probably used to lift the heavy font cover into place.

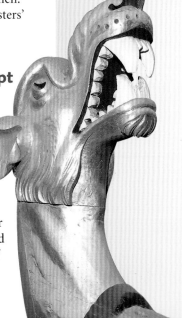

Medieval stained glass

It seems incredible that, despite three major fires over the last 200 years, the stained glass in York Minster, much of it medieval, is among the finest in the country. There are 128 windows in all, including the great east window, which covers an area the size of a tennis court, and the famous rose window in the south transept.

Great east window

This contains the largest area of medieval stained glass in a single window and shows the beginning and ending of the world, using scenes from Genesis and the book of Revelation, the first and last books of the Bible.

Rose window

This window, made around 1500, commemorates the end of the Wars of the Roses, the red and white roses symbolizing the 1486 marriage of Henry VII to Elizabeth of York, which united the houses of York and Lancaster. Most of the window survived the fire of 1984 and has been expertly restored.

Great west window

The great west window, also called the 'Heart of Yorkshire' because of its shape, dates from 1338 and is noted for its flamboyant tracery. Nearby are two other early 14th-century windows. The Bell Founder's window shows the craft of the donor who paid for it, while the Jesse Window details Jesus Christ's family tree.

'Five Sisters' window

The 'Five Sisters' window in the north transept dates from around 1260 and is the oldest complete window in York Minster. So-called because it comprises five 15-metre (50-foot) lancet-shaped sections of silver-green 'grisaille' glass, it is now dedicated to the memory of women who died during two World Wars.

Great east window

Jesse window

Rose window

Minster precincts

Follow the Queen's Path past the statue of Emperor Constantine, sitting imperiously on his bronze throne, around the Minster's east front. Ahead is a black and white timbered building – St William's College. Nearby are the Treasurer's House and the entrance to Dean's Park.

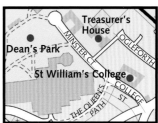

St William's College

Dean's Park

St William's College

St William's College was built in 1461 to house the young chantry priests, who were paid to pray for the souls of their benefactors. The idea was to lodge these often rowdy priests near the watchful Minster staff. The college was named for York's own saint, William Fitzherbert, one-time Archbishop: there's a window dedicated to him in York Minster. Over the centuries the building became derelict but was restored in 1906 by wealthy York businessman Frank Green, who owned the Treasurer's House. The college houses a restaurant and conference centre.

Treasurer's House

This stone Dutch-gabled house, built on the site of the home of the Minster Treasurer, is not what it appears. It was bought by Frank Green in 1897 and 'restored' – each room in the style of a different period. Green collected antiques, redesigning each room to accommodate these treasures. He was obsessive about detail, ensuring that the workmen wore slippers indoors and that each piece of furniture was positioned according to the marks he carefully made on the floor. The Treasurer's House is now looked after by the National Trust.

Dean's Park

You can complete your circuit of the Minster by walking back through Dean's Park, a quiet tree-filled grassy space at the north end of the Minster, or you can go straight to Ogleforth.

Treasurer's House

Goodramgate

Walk past the visitor entrance to the Treasurer's House and along Ogleforth, which will lead you directly to Monk Bar, the grandest of the city entrances, with its four-storey gatehouse and working portcullis. Here you can climb a narrow staircase and walk left to reach Bootham Bar, or right for a shorter walk along the north of the city. The section towards Bootham Bar, built directly over the line of the old Roman wall, takes you past York Minster, giving fine views of its east and north faces and of Dean's Park.

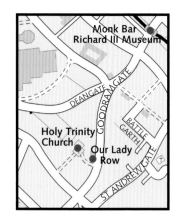

Monk Bar

Richard III Museum

Our Lady Row

Our Lady Row

Goodramgate is said to be named after a Viking leader called Guthrum. On your right is a row of ancient buildings, the upper storey 'jettied' out over the lower, mostly housing shops. This is Our Lady Row, the oldest surviving row of houses in the city. One room deep and two storeys high, the houses were built in 1316 and rented out so that the income from them would pay for masses to be said for the soul of one Thomas Langtoft, a merchant in the city.

Richard III Museum

William Shakespeare's Richard III was a manipulative, scheming, murderous hunchback. He certainly had a bad press. Richard reigned for just over two years, between 1483 and 1485, and is said to have murdered his nephews, the famous 'Princes in the Tower', but was he really as black-hearted as he was portrayed? Find out more by visiting the Richard III Museum, at the top of Monk Bar staircase. Here you'll also learn about the turbulent years of the Wars of the Roses and see the horribly claustrophobic Little Ease prison cell, used for the incarceration of stubborn Roman Catholics.

Holy Trinity Church

Just past Our Lady Row is a narrow entrance leading to what at first appears to be a peaceful garden. This is where you'll find Holy Trinity Church – mainly 15th century, cool and dark, and noted for its stained glass and unusual boxed pews. The floors are a little uneven and the light, filtered through the windows, gives a feeling of tranquillity. The garden that surrounds the church is a leafy haven in the midst of the busy city.

Holy Trinity Church

Walls and bars

York's walls have been torn down in places, but they still encircle the city for almost 3 miles (5 kilometres). You can climb onto their wide walkways at any of the four main 'bars', the medieval entrance gates. Bootham, Micklegate, Walmgate and Monk Bars still exist, offering access for walkers. The Romans were the first to protect their garrison with defensive walls, but what we see today was built mostly in the 12th and 13th centuries.

The Shambles

Walk up Goodramgate into King's Square and take the little twisting lane in the right-hand corner. Ahead is a narrow street, the houses appearing to lean drunkenly towards each other in a higgledy-piggledy fashion, the top storeys of some seeming almost to touch. This is the Shambles, now full of specialist shops.

King's Square

Visitors and locals gather here to rest and refresh themselves. The tombstones in the pavement are clues that this area was once the graveyard of Christ Church.

The Shambles

The word 'shambles', meaning a complete muddle, derives from an early word for a slaughterhouse, and this is what York's most famous

King's Square

and charming street once housed. A clue to the occupation of its medieval tradesmen are the wide runnels in the roadway to allow the blood to flow away and the fastenings for the wooden ledges (known as 'skamels' or 'shammels') on which the freshly slaughtered meat was displayed. It's mentioned in the Domesday Book and is often said to be Europe's best-preserved medieval street.

Shrine to Margaret Clitherow

Halfway down the Shambles, on the right-hand side, you'll find a shrine to Margaret Clitherow, a butcher's wife and a committed Roman Catholic at a time when they were persecuted for their faith. She was tried for celebrating mass and sheltering Jesuit priests in her attic. She refused to plead and, for this, was executed in 1586 by being crushed to death under a heavy door weighted with stones. She was canonized in 1970.

Margaret Clitherow's shrine

The
SHRINE
of The Saint
MARGARET CLITHEROW
✝

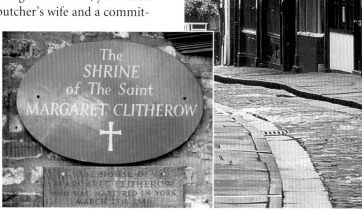

The Shambles

DIG

Here you can grab a trowel and get down to it – find out what it's really like to be an archaeologist and literally uncover more of York's buried history. York Archaeological Trust launched the innovative DIG adventure at St Saviour's Church in St Saviourgate in early 2006. Visitors of all ages may dig, survey, map sites and try their hands at reconstruction.

DIG

Whip-Ma-Whop-Ma-Gate

People come here to look at the sign of this, York's shortest street, squashed between Pavement (said to be the first paved footway in the city) and the Stonebow. There are disagreements about the origin of the name. Was this where people (or dogs) were publicly whipped? Or perhaps it is a medieval expression of scorn, which translates roughly as 'Call this a street!'

Newgate Market

York's daily market with its dozens of busy stalls selling fresh produce, flowers, fish, meat and clothes is one of the best open-air markets in the country.

Chocolate – York's Sweet Story

What better way to discover York's chocolate-making past than by indulging your sweet tooth? Learn about everyone's favourite chocolate to take a break with, the Kit Kat, and your favourite stocking-filler, Terry's Chocolate Orange, and how the confectionery giants behind them contributed to York's Heritage in this exciting modern visitor experience. Not forgetting the behind-the-scenes look into the lives of the men and women who worked to make these chocolate creations.

Newgate Market

Coppergate

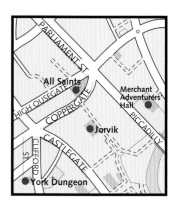

Coppergate is one of York's main shopping areas, but just below today's busy streets is an earlier world. Here the heart of Jorvik, the capital of the Viking's northern kingdom and a thriving community more than 1,100 years ago, has been recreated.

Jorvik Viking Centre

Jorvik Viking Centre

In the late 1970s archaeologists couldn't believe their eyes when they uncovered the remains of a beautifully preserved Viking street. Now you can see it for yourself at the hugely popular and innovative Jorvik Viking Centre. Below the pavements of present-day Coppergate a time car takes you back through the centuries to the Viking city as it was one day in AD 975. You'll never forget what you see, hear and smell.

All Saints Church, Pavement

This mainly 14th-century church is unmissable because of its tall and elegant lantern tower rising above the streets of Coppergate and High Ousegate. This was where, nightly, a bright light would shine to guide weary travellers through the dangerous Forest of Galtres into the safety of the city. There is a fine 13th-century sanctuary knocker in the shape of a lion's head and the church has its own ghost story: a glamorous young curly-headed woman ghost, dressed in a shroud, is said to have met mourners at the door when funerals were being held.

All Saints Church

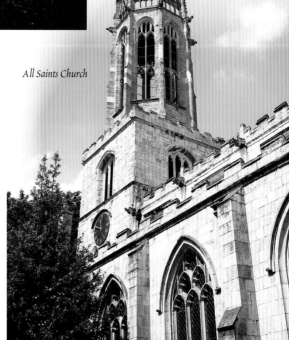

The Merchant Adventurers' Hall

This half-timbered building is one of the finest examples of a medieval guildhall in Europe. In the Middle Ages the life of a great city was controlled by the guild companies. York, a large port, had more than 50 merchant and craft guilds, none more powerful than the Merchant Adventurers, who controlled the cloth trade. This was their hall, built between 1357 and 1361. In the undercroft, evidence of their charity exists – here was a hospital where the needy of the city were cared for. The great hall is enormous, with huge timbers supporting the roof. There is a chapel as well.

Dick Turpin

Dick Turpin's grave lies in what was once the churchyard of St George's Church, near Walmgate Bar. The headstone reads 'Richard Palmer, alias Richard Turpin, notorious highwayman and horse stealer'.

The Merchant Adventurers' Hall

York Dungeon

If you misbehaved in York in medieval times the chances are you would have faced some grisly and probably fatal punishment. Gruesome events happen underground and the Dungeon, located below Clifford Street, displays brandings, boilings, beheadings, roastings and drownings. The story of highwayman Dick Turpin is told here, as is that of another York miscreant – Guy Fawkes.

Viking joiners and turners

The name Coppergate derives from the Viking 'Kopparigat', which means the street of the joiners and turners and gives a clue to the nature of the community hundreds of years ago.

Parliament Street

The pedestrianized tree-lined centre of this wide street plays host to entertainers and pavement games, while there are plenty of seats for those who are in need of a bit of a rest.

Parliament Street

Castle precincts

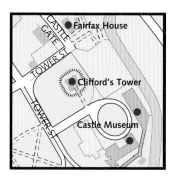

York's massive castle once stood just a step away from Coppergate, down Castlegate. William the Conqueror first built a wooden castle here on a raised mound in 1068. Two hundred years later Henry III completed a stone structure, the remains of which stand as Clifford's Tower, a wonderful vantage point over the city. The cluster of buildings below, constructed on other parts of the castle remains, have all played important parts in the history of York. This large oval area is imaginatively named the Eye of York by the locals.

Clifford's Tower

The prominent tower with its chapel on the first floor is now in the care of English Heritage and is almost all that remains of the once enormous castle built by Henry III between 1244 and 1270. The parapet, 24 metres (80 feet) above ground level, gives excellent views. Tragedy occurred here one night in 1190 when around 150 Jewish people took refuge from a violent mob. Most chose to take their own lives to avoid being massacred.

Clifford's Tower

Castle Museum

This wonderful collection is Britain's most popular folk museum. It was started in a small way by Dr Kirk, a local country doctor, who 'rescued' everyday household objects destined for the rubbish tip. His collection found its way to the old Female Prison, which opened as the Castle Museum in 1938. The museum's collection grew rapidly and, since 1952, has occupied the Debtors' Prison, too. The

Castle Museum

most famous exhibit is the recreated Victorian street, Kirkgate, and Half Moon Court, built in the crescent shape of the old prison yard. Here you can see Edwardian York as it must have been in the first decade of the 20th century. Here too is the cell from the old County Gaol, later the Debtors' Prison, in which dastardly Dick Turpin was incarcerated before he was taken to Tyburn, near today's racecourse, to be hanged.

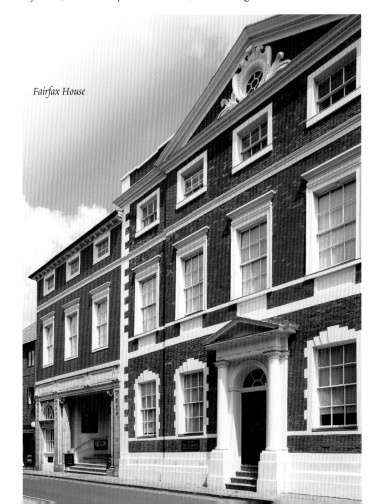

Fairfax House

Fairfax House

This fine restoration of a Georgian gentleman's house is a triumph of survival over tribulation. Thanks to the York Civic Trust and architect Francis Johnson, the building, which had slipped into use as a dance hall, a yoga studio and a café, is now probably the finest example of a Georgian house in Britain. Designed by John Carr of York (whose portrait hangs in the library) for Viscount Fairfax and his daughter, Anne, the house was built in 1745 and decorated in the following decade.

Terry's of York

For more than 200 years Terry's chocolate was made in York, but in September 2005 the site closed and production moved abroad. There's still a link to the family at Fairfax House, where the priceless collection of clocks and furniture once belonging to the late Noel Terry (who introduced Terry's chocolate orange) is housed. You can also visit Terry's former home Goddards, now a National Trust property.

Museum Gardens

These peaceful 4 hectares (10 acres), where you may walk, sit and picnic, were once part of St Mary's Abbey. The site was bought by the York Philosophical Society as a private scientific and botanical resource, but is now York's main public park, much used and well loved.

St Mary's Abbey and hospitium

You'll see people walking and sitting around the elegant stone arches that, along with walls that run along Bootham Bar and Marygate, are all that remain of what was once the wealthiest Benedictine monastery in the North. Henry VIII was to blame for its dissolution although the stones did not go to waste – they were used to build the Ouse Bridge and the County Gaol. This area once contained granaries, stables, a brewhouse and a bakehouse, a mill, a fish house and a tailor's workshop. They have all disappeared except for the 13th-century hospitium, the Abbey guesthouse. This two-storey building, with lower walls of stone and timber on the upper level, is still used for functions.

The hospitium

Multangular Tower

There were once eight of these ten-sided multangular towers built into the walls of the Roman defences. The lower 6 metres (19 feet) contain original stonework.

St Mary's Abbey

The Observatory

This octagonal building, constructed in 1831, contains what was once the biggest refracting telescope in the world. The telescope was built in 1850 by Thomas Cooke and is still used on occasions.

St Olave's Church

Just behind the abbey ruins is the lovely St Olave's Church, founded by Siward, a Danish earl, in 1050. The York artist William Etty (see page 22) is buried here.

St Olave's Church

Yorkshire Museum

Here you will find the history of York covering 2,000 years in treasures from the Romans, the Vikings and the rich medieval period. One visit is probably not enough to see the permanent collections, which include fossilized dinosaurs, work of 20th-century artists, and special exhibitions, which change regularly. In 1985 an exquisite, ornate engraved gold and sapphire pendant was found using a metal detector in the Yorkshire town of Middleham. The Middleham jewel, said by some to have belonged to Richard III, is now safely in the museum.

Middleham jewel

King's Staith

River Ouse

Today pleasure boats cruise the wide River Ouse, but in the past York was a great port whose wealth relied on its river, easily navigable from the wide mouth of the Humber. You can reach the riverbanks from Museum Gardens and enjoy the views to Lendal Bridge on your left and Scarborough Bridge to the right. Lower down the river, King's and Queen's Staiths are where laden vessels once unloaded. Now you can sit, drink and eat on King's Staith.

River trade

'No city in England is better furnished with provisions of every kind, not any so cheap, the river being so navigable, and so near the sea, the merchants here trade directly to what part of the world they will.'

Daniel Defoe, 1724

Exhibition Square

Walking tours and open top buses start their sightseeing trips here and many of York's grand old buildings are clustered near the elegant fountains of the square.

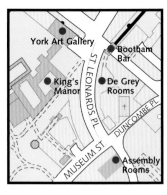

Bootham Bar

This was one of the four main entrances to the medieval walled city and is the oldest gateway, parts of it dating back to the 11th or 12th centuries. It is the only bar to be built on or near one of the principal Roman entrances to York. There is easy access to the walls here and a walk round to Monk Bar gives wonderful views over York Minster.

Bootham Bar

King's Manor

King's Manor

A classic old building is set back off the square, at right angles to York Art Gallery. This is King's Manor, once the house of the abbot of St Mary's Abbey. After the abbey was destroyed, the manor was taken over in 1561 by the Crown. During the English Civil War, Charles I set up his headquarters here and the building was attacked in 1642. Now it belongs to York University and serves as the department of archaeology. Visitors may look at the courtyards and some of the interior, and enjoy lunch in the refectory.

Assembly Rooms

You can still visit this building on Blake Street, the heart of York's social life in the 18th century, but only if you feel hungry. The Assembly Rooms opened in 1732 and here, where people once dressed in their best to dance and play cards, they now eat Italian food. Another of York's splendid old buildings has also become a restaurant: the former gentleman's club in Museum Street is today a grand pizza parlour.

York Art Gallery

Cheerful fountains and a larger-than-life statue of the painter William Etty, noted for his splendid nudes, make an impressive frontage for York's art gallery. The Gallery is currently undergoing refurbishment and a facelift, but will reopen in 2015 with more galleries, bigger gardens and a new Centre for British Studio Ceramics. Across the road are the elegant De Grey Rooms, opened in 1842 as the Officers' Mess for the Yorkshire Hussar Regiment.

Roman streets

High and Low Petergate are the streets that take you directly across York from Bootham Bar, the northern entrance. Petergate follows the line of the Via Principalis, the main Roman route through York, while Stonegate, leading directly to York Minster, follows the old Via Praetoria from the River Ouse.

Assembly Rooms

Railway museum

The National Railway Museum, which tells the story of the railways since the 19th century and displays many iconic locomotives, is the lure for many who visit York. The museum is behind York's railway station, itself a well-preserved example of elegant Victorian architecture and a hub for much of today's railway traffic.

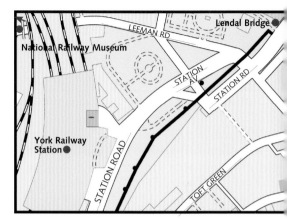

Lendal Bridge

This is the bridge you'll cross to enter the city if you arrive by train. The ornate and Gothic decorations on this iron bridge include the white rose of York, shields depicting the lions of England and the crossed keys of the diocese of York. Lendal Tower and Barkers Tower on the north and south sides of the River Ouse once acted as toll houses, extracting payment from traders travelling up the river. The first Lendal Bridge collapsed in 1860 during construction, killing five people. Today's bridge was designed by Thomas Page – designer of London's Westminster Bridge – and completed in 1863.

Flying Scotsman

Flying Scotsman

The world-famous locomotive has been restored to her full mainline running condition, so that she can once again pull trains around the UK. 'The Flying Scotsman Story' exhibition can be enjoyed at the museum and, from time to time, the locomotive can also be seen here. She was purchased for the nation in 2004 with public donations and money from the National Heritage Memorial Fund.

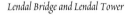

Lendal Bridge and Lendal Tower

National Railway Museum

Steam rides, pulled by Rocket

York Railway Station

On your way through the station take a few minutes to admire Thomas Prosser and William Peachey's fine architecture – well-preserved colonnades, and elegant arches – built in 1873–77. When first built, the station had 13 platforms and was the largest in the world.

National Railway Museum

More than 100 historic locomotives and an abundance of railway memorabilia, including over 290 items of rolling stock, are displayed in three halls situated in Leeman Road, close to York's railway station. Here you'll see the 1938 Mallard, once the fastest steam engine in the world, a Japanese Bullet Train, the only one of its kind outside Japan, and locomotives dating back to 1829.

Giants of steam cluster around a genuine turntable. Of particular interest is the luxurious 'Palaces on Wheels' exhibition, showing royal trains.

The museum has extensive archives of railway posters, railway-inspired art and film, as well as displays showing how the railways were built, run and used.

Children will love the interactive railway stories about special train journeys leaving London for the north. Clickety Clack and Quick! The Queen is Coming are designed for very young children. A miniature railway provides a ride around the site. A replica of Stephenson's Rocket is based at the museum, often used for steam train rides in the school holidays.

Visitors wishing to see a specific railway vehicle are advised to contact the museum before making their journey. Some vehicles are in full working condition and regularly service the mainline or travel to heritage railways.

See how royals travelled through the ages in Station Hall

Micklegate Bar

Complete your walk back to St Helen's Square by re-entering the city through Micklegate Bar – the one traditionally used by royalty, visiting dignitaries and very important visitors. On the way you can visit a convent with a difference.

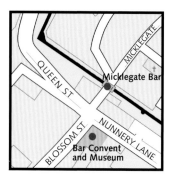

Micklegate Bar

This rectangular gatehouse, topped by three storeys, was the most important of York's gateways. Even today, Her Majesty the Queen has to stop at Micklegate Bar to ask permission from the Lord Mayor before she may enter the city. It's where the severed heads of traitors were skewered on pikestaffs and displayed from the roof of the bar to be pecked by crows and magpies. They were often left to rot for as long as eight or nine years. A small museum tells the story.

Bar Convent and Museum

This is the oldest convent still functioning in England, and one of the most enterprising. When a challenge was thrown down in 1686 to found a school for girls, the nuns set up an educational establishment that functioned until 1985. Now the convent is a guest house, has a conference centre, museum, café and shop. It welcomes visitors who want to stay in the guest house, eat, or simply visit the museum and the lovely buildings, including the chapel.

Alas, poor York

'Off with his head and set it on York gates; so York may overlook the town of York.' Queen Margaret in Shakespeare's *Henry VI*

Bar Convent Museum   *Micklegate Bar*

Information

What's on

Full and up-to-date information on all events in the city can be found at the Visitor Information Centre (p. 28).

January–February
Pantomime, Theatre Royal

February
Jorvik Viking Festival;
York RAG Charity Procession

May–October
York Races

June
Lord Mayor's Parade;
Late Music Festival

July
Early Music Festival
Festival of the Rivers

August
Ebor, York Racecourse;
Yorkshire Air Show

September
York National Book Fair;
Festival of Food and Drink

November
St Nicholas' Christmas Fair

December
Festival of Angels;
Pantomime, Theatre Royal

Jorvik Viking Festival

Museums and galleries

Castle Museum
01904 687687, www.yorkcastlemuseum.org.uk;
Micklegate Bar Museum
01904 615 505,
www.micklegatebar.com;
National Railway Museum
0844 815 3139,
www.nrm.org.uk;
Richard III Experience
01904 615505,
www.richardiiiexperience.com
York Art Gallery
01904 687687,
www.yorkartgallery.org.uk;
Yorkshire Museum &
Gardens 01904 687687,
www.yorkshiremuseum.org.uk

Tours and trips

Information on the following tours, and many others, can be found at the Visitor Information Centre or on www.visityork.org.

Walking tours leave daily from various points in the city. There are a variety of other walks including ghost tours, pub tours and a brewery visit.

Open-top bus tours run frequently during the day leaving from Exhibition Square. You may hop on or off at any of the 21 stops.

River boats depart regularly from Lendal Bridge, Kings Staith (Ouse Bridge) and Skeldergate Bridge.

Jorvik Festival

February might be the bleakest of all months in the rest of the country, but in York you'll find the city full of colour, spectacle and drama as they celebrate the annual Jorvik Viking Festival. Join experts and enthusiasts in a family-friendly, nine-day celebration of York's Viking history, using storytelling, feasting, historic walks, traditional crafts, battles and a longboat race on the River Ouse.

Ebor Festival

This is the highlight of the second half of the flat racing season, held at York Racecourse. Often called the 'Ascot of the North', Ebor combines fashion with top-class racing over an exciting three days in August.

Mystery plays

In medieval days the city guilds would perform a cycle of 48 plays at Corpus Christi (in July). These mystery plays tell the stories of the Bible from the Creation to the Last Judgement. They are still performed in the city regularly, by a cast of more than 200 actors and musicians.

Front cover: York Minster
Back cover: The Shambles

Acknowledgements

Photography © Pitkin Publishing by Neil Jinkerson. Additional photography by kind permission of Alamy: 14b inset (Paul M Thompson); Bridgeman Art Library: 17tr; www.britain-onview.com: 12l; Collections: 10r; Alan Curtis: 17br; Dean & Chapter of York: 8cr, 9br, 10ct and b; FotoLibra: 18 (Andrew Birtwhistle); iStock: FC; National Railway Museum: 24c, 25tr, 25b; Peter Gray: 5cl, 7cr; Pitkin Publishing: 9tr, 14/15 (Peter Gray), 24bl (Derek Forss); National Trust Photo Library: 11br (Bill Batten); Shutterstock/ Shanna Hyatt: BC; York Archaeological Trust: 15tr, 16cl, 27bl; York Castle Museum: 19t; York Museums Trust: 21tr.

The publishers would like to thank Rebecca Francis and Blue Badge guide Larch Cardona for their assistance in the preparation of this guide.

Written by Annie Bullen; the author has asserted her moral rights.
Edited by Angela Royston.
Designed by Simon Borrough.
Picture research by Jan Kean.
City map/park & ride map by The Map Studio, Romsey, Hants, UK; walk maps by Simon Borrough; maps based on cartography © George Philip Ltd.

Publication in this form © Pitkin Publishing 2007, latest reprint 2017.

Printed in Turkey.
ISBN 978-1-84165-192-7   6/17

i **York Visitor Information Centre**
1 Museum Street
York YO1 7DT
tel: 01904 554455
email: info@visityork.org
website: www.visityork.org

Shopmobility
For the loan of manual or electric wheelchairs and powered scooters to those who need them.
Level 2, Piccadilly Car Park (above Topshop, Piccadilly)
To book, tel: 01904 679222

PITKIN CITY GUIDES

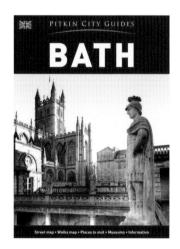

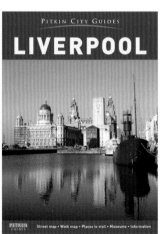

This guide is just one in a series of city titles

Available by mail order.
See our website, **www.pavilionbooks.com**, for our full range of titles, or contact us for a copy of our brochure.

Pitkin Publishing, Pavilion Books Company Limited, 43 Great Ormond Street, London WC1N 3HZ

Enquiries and sales: +44 (0)20 7462 1509
Email: sales@pavilionbooks.com